MASTERING YOUR

SAMSUNG GALAXY S24+

A COMPREHENSIVE USER
GUIDE

Sean M. Richards

MASTERING YOUR SAMSUNG GALAXY S24+

TABLE OF CONTENTS

INTRODUCTION

"Mastering Your Samsung Galaxy S24+: A Comprehensive User Guide" is where you are now. This book is intended to be your reliable travel companion while you explore the Samsung Galaxy S24+, whether you are a new owner or hoping to realize all of its potential.

We cover every facet of the Samsung Galaxy S24+ in our extensive user manual, giving you precise guidance to enable you to use its functions with ease. Our goal is to enable you to reap the maximum benefits from your smartphone, starting from the basic setup and personalization and continuing through advanced settings, troubleshooting, and beyond.

With its cutting-edge features and capabilities, the Galaxy S24+ is at the forefront of technological advancements. We'll go over the features of the gadget in this guide, along with some helpful hints and techniques to improve your output, inventiveness, and general user experience.

The level of competence covered by "Mastering Your Samsung Galaxy S24+" is suitable for both casual and tech-advanced users. Together, let's set out on this adventure to make sure you fully grasp the possibilities of the Samsung Galaxy S24+. Savor exploring and learning all that this amazing gadget has to offer!

CHAPTER 1

WELCOME TO THE SAMSUNG GALAXY S24+

Cheers to your newfound ownership of the Samsung Galaxy S24+! You've stepped into the world of cutting edge technology, where style and innovation coexist. The Galaxy S24+ is more than simply a phone; it's a doorway to an infinitely fascinating world.

With its svelte frame, breathtaking display, and potent performance, the Galaxy S24+ redefines what is possible for a smartphone. This gadget is made to enhance every part of your digital life, whether you're using it to stay in touch with friends and family, capture amazing moments with its sophisticated camera system, or lose yourself in your favorite entertainment.

MASTERING YOUR SAMSUNG GALAXY S24+

There are a ton of features and capabilities on the Samsung Galaxy S24+ that are just waiting to be discovered when you set out on your adventure with it. With its user-friendly design, strong security features, and cutting-edge tools, this gadget is made to fit your demands and improve your everyday life.

The Galaxy S24+ is here to surpass your expectations, whether you're a tech enthusiast trying to test the limits of what your smartphone can accomplish or someone who is just looking for a trustworthy partner for daily tasks.

Welcome, then, to the community for the Samsung Galaxy S24+! Prepare to explore new frontiers, increase productivity, and unleash your creativity with a gadget that's way ahead of its time.

1.1. Overview Of The New Features

With the Samsung Galaxy S24+, you may enjoy a plethora of innovative features that are sure to transform your smartphone usage. Here's an overview of what makes this gadget unique:

Innovative Camera Technology: The Galaxy S24+'s upgraded camera features, such as its sophisticated image stabilization, AI-driven scene optimization, and better low-light performance, let you take beautiful pictures and videos in any situation.

Immersive Display: The immersive Dynamic AMOLED display of the Galaxy S24+ allows you to see images like never before. This display guarantees that every image and video comes to life with remarkable clarity and detail thanks to its deep blacks, bright colors, and HDR10+ compatibility.

Enhanced Performance: Whether you're gaming, streaming media, or multitasking, the Galaxy S24+'s powerful combination of the newest chipset and lots of RAM allows for blazing-fast performance. Additionally, you'll have plenty of room to keep all of your pictures, videos, and apps thanks to the increased storage options.

Advanced Security Features: Use Knox security platform, fingerprint scanning, facial recognition, and other advanced security features to safeguard your personal data. Whether you're unlocking your device or conducting online purchases, you can be confident that your data is secure.

Simple User Interface: The Galaxy S24+'s simple user interface makes it easy to navigate around the device. You may customize your smartphone with features like One UI, smart gestures, and configurable app layouts to fit your needs and expedite your productivity.

Seamless Connectivity: The Galaxy S24+'s extensive connectivity choices allow you to stay connected no matter where you travel. With features like Wi-Fi 6E compatibility for better wireless performance and 5G support for lightning-fast internet connections, this device makes sure you're always connected to the outside world.

Extended Battery Life: The Galaxy S24+'s extended battery life allows you to wave goodbye to worries about running out of power. No matter how hard your responsibilities are, you can stay fueled up all day with quick charging capabilities and clever battery management features.

Just a handful of the fascinating new features available on the Samsung Galaxy S24+ are listed here. This gadget will improve all facets of your digital life with its innovative technology, stylish appearance, and intuitive functionality.

CHAPTER 2

GETTING STARTED

Greetings from the fascinating Samsung Galaxy S24+ world! The first step to realizing the full potential of your new device is to get it going. In order to configure your Galaxy S24+ and start your trip, simply follow these steps:

Unboxing: Carefully open the Galaxy S24+'s packaging when you first receive it to make sure all of the attachments are inside. These usually consist of the user handbook, SIM ejector tool, charging cord, and power adapter.

SIM Card Installation: To install your SIM card on your new Galaxy S24+, remove the SIM card tray using the SIM ejector tool. As directed by the instructions, place your SIM card into the tray and then put the tray back into the device.

Power On: To turn on the device, press and hold the power button on its side. To start the setup procedure, adhere to the on-screen instructions.

Language and location: From the list of possibilities, choose the language and location that you like. By doing this, you can make sure that the settings on your Galaxy S24+ reflect your preferences.

Connect to Wi-Fi: Choose your Wi-Fi network from the list of accessible networks, then, if prompted, enter your password to enable internet access. As an alternative, you might decide to establish a mobile data connection at a later time.

Log in to Your Samsung Account: To access extra features and services, such Galaxy Store apps and

Samsung Cloud backup, if you have a Samsung account, sign in. During the setup procedure, you can create a Samsung account if you don't already have one.

Google Account Setup: To access Google services like Gmail, Drive, and the Play Store, log in using your Google account. You can either skip this step and add an account later, or you can establish a Google account if you don't already have one.

Device Security: To safeguard your device and personal information, set up security features like a fingerprint scan, PIN, or screen lock pattern. Select a technique that offers sufficient security and is convenient for you.

Personalization: Select your preferred theme, background, and app arrangement to make your Galaxy S24+ uniquely yours. To fit your tastes, you may also change settings like notification preferences, speaker volume, and display brightness.

Backup and Restore: You can use Google Backup or Samsung Smart Switch to move contacts, pictures, apps, and other data to your new Galaxy S24+ if you're moving from an old device. To finish the transfer process, adhere to the on-screen directions.

After completing these instructions, you can use your Samsung Galaxy S24+! Make the most of your new gadget by exploring its features and downloading your favorite apps. Check the user manual or contact Samsung customer care if you have any problems or need assistance. Have fun with your Galaxy S24+!

2.1. Opening And First Setup

After unpacking and configuring your new Samsung Galaxy S24+, start your adventure. Here's a step-by-step tutorial to get you going:

Unpack Your Galaxy S24+: Take the Galaxy S24+ out of its packing with care, making sure that all of the accessories are there. These usually consist of the user handbook, SIM ejector tool, charging cord, and power adapter.

Examine the Contents: Take a moment to look through the box's contents to make sure everything is present and in working order. For assistance, get in touch with Samsung customer service or the shop if you find any missing or damaged items.

Insert the SIM card: To transfer your current SIM card to your new Galaxy S24+, remove the SIM card tray using the SIM ejector tool. As directed by the instructions, place your SIM card into the tray and then put the tray back into the device.

Turn On Your Device: To turn on your device, press and hold the power button on the side. When the Galaxy

S24+ boots up, wait for the setup to start, then follow the on-screen instructions.

Select Language and location: From the list of possibilities, select the language and location that you like. By doing this, you can make sure that the settings on your Galaxy S24+ reflect your preferences.

Connect to a Wi-Fi or mobile network: Choose your Wi-Fi network from the list of networks that are available, and if prompted, enter your password to allow internet access. As an alternative, you might decide to establish a mobile data connection at a later time.

Log in to Your Samsung Account: To access extra features and services, such Galaxy Store apps and Samsung Cloud backup, if you have a Samsung account, sign in. During the setup procedure, you can create a Samsung account if you don't already have one.

Google Account Setup: To access Google services like Gmail, Drive, and the Play Store, log in using your Google account. You can either skip this step and add an account later, or you can establish a Google account if you don't already have one.

Configure Device Security: To safeguard your device and personal information, select a screen lock technique like a pattern, PIN, password, or fingerprint scan. Pick a technique that offers sufficient security and is convenient for you.

Customize Your Device: Choose the wallpaper, theme, and app arrangement that you want to use on your Galaxy S24+. To fit your tastes, you may also change settings like notification preferences, speaker volume, and display brightness.

Transfer Data from Previous Device: To move your contacts, pictures, apps, and other data to your new Galaxy S24+, you can utilize Google Backup or

Samsung Smart Switch. To finish the transfer process, adhere to the on-screen directions.

Examine and Agree to the Terms: In order to continue with the setup procedure, go over and agree to the terms and conditions for using your Galaxy S24+.

After completing these instructions, you can use your Samsung Galaxy S24+! Make the most of your new gadget by exploring its features and downloading your favorite apps. Check the user manual or contact Samsung customer care if you have any problems or need assistance. Have fun with your Galaxy S24+!

2.2. Configuring Essential Settings

It's time to adjust the necessary settings on your Samsung Galaxy S24+ after you've unboxed and set it up to suit your needs and tastes. This article will assist you in configuring these settings:

To access the Settings app on your Galaxy S24+, swipe down from the top of the screen and hit the gear icon in the notification panel, or tap the gear icon in the app drawer.

Network and Internet: Under the "Connections" or "Network & Internet" section, configure Wi-Fi, mobile data, and other network options. Configure mobile hotspots, VPNs, and Wi-Fi calling based on your preferences.

Display Settings: To enhance your viewing experience, change the brightness, screen timeout, and screen resolution. Tailor the screen mode, font size, and Always On Display settings to your liking.

Sound and Vibration: Under the "Sounds and vibration" or "Sound" area, adjust the sound and vibration settings. Change the vibration intensity, notification sound, and ringtone. Turn on or off the keyboard, screen lock, and touch noises.

Control alerts, texts, and app notifications using this feature. Set up custom notification settings for priority, sound, vibration, and badges.

Battery and Device Care: Refer to the "Battery" or "Device Care" section to keep an eye on battery usage and improve battery performance. To extend the life of your battery, turn on battery saver mode, adaptive battery, and optimize settings.

Security and Privacy: By establishing security settings, you can guarantee the safety of your device and personal information. Install screen lock techniques including pattern, password, PIN, or biometric (fingerprint or face recognition) authentication. Turn on safe startup, find my mobile, and other security features.

Accounts and Backup: Go to the "Accounts" or "Cloud and accounts" area to manage the accounts connected to your Galaxy S24+. Change the accounts for Samsung, Google, and other companies. Set up backup and restoration options to protect your information.

Enhance accessibility for people with impairments by personalizing accessibility settings. To suit your accessibility needs, change settings for vision, hearing, interaction, and dexterity.

Advanced Features: To improve your experience with the Galaxy S24+, explore the advanced features and settings. Set up features like Edge panels, Smart Pop-up View, Bixby routines, and more.

Additional device settings, including language and input, date and time, and software updates, can be customized. Modify the time zone, date format, keyboard, and language settings.

Concerning Phone: See details about your Galaxy S24+, including the software version, model number, and current state of the device. To make sure your device is up to date, check for software updates and run system updates.

You may customize your Samsung Galaxy S24+ to fit your tastes and maximize its performance to meet your demands by adjusting these crucial settings. Proceed to explore the settings menu to find more features and customization choices to improve your overall experience.

2.3. Transferring Information into Your Galaxy S24+

Transferring data from your previous Samsung Galaxy S24+ will help you set up your new phone more quickly and ensure that all of your crucial data is at your fingertips. To transfer data to your Galaxy S24+, follow these steps:

With Samsung Smart Switch, you can wirelessly or via a cable move data from your old handset to the Galaxy S24+. It's a very handy feature. To transfer data using the Samsung Smart Switch, take these steps:

From the Google Play Store or Galaxy Store, download and install the Samsung Smart Switch app on your old device and the Galaxy S24+.
Select the proper transfer method (Cable or Wireless) when you open the Smart Switch app on both devices. To connect the devices, adhere to the directions displayed on the screen.
Select the data categories you wish to move, including contacts, messages, images, videos, apps, and more.
Check that everything moved successfully by looking over the transferred data on your Galaxy S24+ when the transfer is finished.
Google Data Protect: You may quickly restore your data on your Galaxy S24+ if you have backed it up to

your Google account. To restore data using Google Backup, take these steps:

Make sure you log in with the same Google account you used to backup your data while setting up your Galaxy S24+.

To configure your device's options and settings, adhere to the on-screen instructions.

Choose to restore from your Google account when asked to restore data.

Select which backup to recover from and what kinds of data, including contacts, calendar events, app data, and more, to restore.

Your Galaxy S24+ will be able to access your data after the restoration process is finished.

Alternative Techniques: As an alternative, you can manually transmit data using techniques like:

SD Card: From your previous smartphone, transfer images, videos, and other files to a microSD card. Then, put the microSD card into the Galaxy S24+ and continue to transfer files.

USB Cable: Use a USB cable to connect your old device to the Galaxy S24+ so you can move files between the two devices on your computer.

Cloud Storage: You can download data to your Galaxy S24+ after uploading it to cloud storage services like Dropbox, Google Drive, or Samsung Cloud.

Regardless of the approach you take, backing up data to your Samsung Galaxy S24+ guarantees that all of your crucial information is always close at hand, making the switch to a new device easy and painless.

CHAPTER 3

NAVIGATING THE INTERFACE

You can easily navigate and access all of the features and functionalities of your Samsung Galaxy S24+ thanks to its intuitive and user-friendly UI. Here's a guide to help you efficiently use the interface:

Home Screen: Your device's home screen is where you'll find all of your favorite shortcuts, widgets, and apps. You can swipe up from the bottom of the screen or click the Home button to go back to the Home screen from any app or screen.

App Drawer: Every installed app on your device is stored in the App Drawer. Swipe up from the Home screen to open the App Drawer. You may search for apps, reorganize app icons, and organize your apps with folders from this location.

Quick Settings Panel: This panel offers instant access to toggles and important settings. Swipe down once with one finger or two fingers from the top of the screen to open the Quick Settings window. You may adjust Wi-Fi, Bluetooth, and screen brightness from this location.

Notifications: Notifications show information about emails, incoming messages, app changes, and more. They are displayed at the top of the screen. Use one finger to swipe down from the top of the screen to view alerts. Notifications can be dismissed or acted upon by swiping left or right.

Navigation Gestures: To swiftly navigate the interface, the Galaxy S24+ has a number of navigation gestures. To reach the recent applications screen, for instance, swipe up from the bottom of the screen; to switch between recent apps, swipe left or right on the Home button; and to view the notification panel, swipe down on the fingerprint sensor.

Edge Panels: These panels offer instant access to contacts, applications, tools, and other resources. Swipe inward from the screen's edge when in an app or on the Home screen to access Edge Panels. Edge Panels are adaptable to your tastes; you can add or delete panels as needed.

Navigation Buttons: To navigate the UI, the Galaxy S24+ ships with navigation buttons located at the bottom of the screen by default. These buttons are the Recent Apps, Back, and Home buttons. In the device settings, you can change the gestures and arrangement of the navigation bar.

One-handed Mode: You can turn on one-handed mode in the device settings if you'd rather use your device with just one hand. For better one-handed use, this function shrinks the screen and moves it to one side.

You may maximize the capabilities and functionality of your Samsung Galaxy S24+ and traverse the UI with ease if you can grasp these navigation techniques. To further customize the interface to your liking, explore more gestures and customization options in the device settings.

3.1. Crucial Home Screen Items

The main entry point to your Samsung Galaxy S24+'s functionality is its Home screen, which provides easy access to widgets, apps, and other crucial features. The secret to getting the most out of your smartphone is to comprehend and customize the Home screen. This is a summary of the necessary Home screen elements:

App Icons: The installed apps on your device are represented by app icons. To open the associated app, tap on its icon. To improve organization, drag and drop your app icons into folders or other groups on the Home screen.

Widgets: From the Home screen, Widgets are dynamic app extensions that offer instant access to information and functionality. Widgets for the weather, calendar, and music player are a few examples. Long-press on an empty space on the Home screen, then choose "Widgets" from the menu to add a widget.

App Drawer Icon: This icon, which usually appears at the bottom of the Home screen, gives users access to the complete list of all installed applications. You can explore and launch apps that are not already on the Home screen by tapping on the App Drawer icon.

Search Bar: You can easily search for apps, contacts, settings, and more with the Search Bar at the top of the Home screen. You can use the keyboard to type a search query by touching the Search Bar, or you can use the microphone button to record voice commands.

Dock: The Dock is a dedicated space at the bottom of the Home screen that conveniently stores commonly used apps. The Phone, Messages, and Internet browser are frequently used programs that are typically found in the Dock by default. You can rearrange the app icons in the Dock to make it more personalized to your tastes.

Folders: Folders gather together relevant apps to help you manage and tidy your Home screen. Drag one app icon onto another app icon to create a folder. After naming the folder, drag more program icons into it in the desired locations.

Wallpaper and Themes: Add unique wallpapers and themes to make your Home screen uniquely yours. Select from a number of wallpapers that come pre-installed, or use the Galaxy Themes app to get more. To view the wallpaper and theme options, long-press on a blank space on the Home screen.

Notification Badges: To signify unread alerts, notification badges can be seen on app icons. A brief visual cue for fresh emails, messages, or other notifications is provided by these badges. The device settings allow you to change the notification badge configuration.

You can effectively browse and personalize your Samsung Galaxy S24+ Home screen to your liking and maximize productivity by learning these key elements of the Home screen. Try out various backgrounds, widgets, and layouts to make a Home screen that complements your taste and improves your smartphone experience.

3.2. Quick Settings and Notifications

Your Samsung Galaxy S24+ is not complete without notifications and fast settings, which offer instant access to crucial data and device configurations. What you should know about controlling alerts and getting access to

QUICK SETTINGS

Alerts

Information about incoming messages, emails, app updates, and other events is displayed in notifications, which are located at the top of the screen.
To access your notifications and enlarge the notification panel, slide down from the top of the screen with one finger. To close the panel, swipe up.
You can act on a notice by tapping on it, which will open the related app, or you can act right from the notification shade. You can, for instance, ignore an email, respond to a message, or set an alarm to go off later.

Management of Notifications

Long-pressing on a notice or swiping it to the side will display management choices, such as snooze, block, and prioritize.

You can change notification options, such as tone, vibration, and notification badges, by going to Settings > Notifications and customizing the settings for individual apps.

Fast Settings

Quick Settings offer easy access to toggles and settings for frequently used devices. Using two fingers, swipe down from the top of the screen, or one finger, swipe down once to open Quick Settings.

A grid of toggles for functions including Wi-Fi, Bluetooth, mobile data, do not disturb, and more are visible on the Quick Settings panel. A toggle can be tapped to make a feature active or inactive.

Swipe left or right on the Quick Settings panel to view more Quick Settings tiles. By selecting Quick Settings or by hitting the "Edit" button, you can change which tiles are shown.

Volume and Brightness Controls

There are sliders on the Quick Settings panel to change the volume and brightness of the screen. To access advanced brightness settings, scroll down with one finger and then swipe down again on the brightness slider.

You may also utilize the volume keys to display quick access buttons by dragging down on the status bar. This allows you to rapidly access the brightness and volume settings without opening the Quick Settings panel.

Customization of Notification Shade

By selecting Settings > Notifications > Quick Settings, you may alter the notification shade's look and arrangement. Here, you can also rearrange the tiles and adjust the Quick Settings toggles' order.

You may effectively manage your Samsung Galaxy S24+ and easily access crucial information and device settings by becoming proficient with notifications and Quick Settings. Adapt these options to your tastes to make your smartphone experience more efficient.

3.3. Buttons and Gestures for Navigation

It is possible to navigate the Samsung Galaxy S24+'s interface with a combination of buttons and gestures, providing flexibility and ease. Learn how to use the buttons and gestures for navigating here:

Navigation through Gestures

Back Gesture: To go back, swipe inward from the screen's left or right edge. The conventional back button is replaced with this.

Home Gesture: From any app or screen, swipe up from the bottom of the screen to go back to the Home screen.

Recent applications Gesture: To view the recent applications screen, swipe up from the bottom of the screen and hold it down. To navigate between recently opened apps, swipe left or right on the Home button area.

Buttons for navigation

The Galaxy S24+ has navigation buttons at the bottom of the screen by default:

Home Button: Tap to go from any screen or app back to the Home screen.

Press the back button to return to the previous window or application.

Tap the "Recent Apps" button to see and navigate through the recently used apps.

Navigate to Settings > Display > Navigation Bar to change the button layout, order, and type. You can also select between full-screen gestures and navigation buttons.

Gesture Perception

Gesture sensitivity can be changed to fit your needs. To change the sensitivity level, go to Settings > Display > Navigation Bar > Gesture Sensitivity.

Using the Fingerprint Sensor, swipe gestures:

Additionally, you can carry out the following tasks with swipe movements on the fingerprint sensor:

Swipe Down: To access the notification panel, swipe down on the fingerprint sensor.

Swipe Left or Right: Using the fingerprint sensor, swipe left or right to navigate through Gallery photographs and carry out other customisable tasks.

Settings & Accessibility

The Accessibility settings provide more navigation choices for users with accessibility needs or preferences. To improve navigation and usability, check out features like the Assistant menu, One-handed mode, and more. Gaining proficiency with the Samsung Galaxy S24+'s navigation buttons and gestures enables quick and easy communication with the smartphone. Try out a variety of navigation techniques to determine which ones best fit your needs and usage patterns.

CHAPTER 4: ESSENTIAL APPS AND FEATURES

The Samsung Galaxy S24+ comes packed with a range of essential apps and features designed to enhance your productivity, connectivity, and entertainment experience. Here's a guide to some of the must-have apps and features on your device:

Camera: The Galaxy S24+ boasts a powerful camera system, allowing you to capture stunning photos and videos. Explore features such as Pro mode, Night mode, Portrait mode, and more to unleash your creativity and capture memorable moments.

Messaging and Calling: Stay connected with friends, family, and colleagues using the built-in messaging and calling apps. Send text messages, make voice calls, and video calls using apps like Messages and Phone.

Email and Productivity Apps: Manage your emails and stay productive on the go with apps like Email and

Calendar. Access your work or personal email accounts, schedule appointments, and set reminders to stay organized and efficient.

Internet Browser: Browse the web seamlessly with the pre-installed internet browser, whether you're searching for information, reading articles, or shopping online. Enjoy features such as tabbed browsing, private browsing mode, and bookmarks for easy access to your favorite sites.

Social Media Apps: Stay connected with your social circle using apps like Facebook, Instagram, Twitter, and more. Share updates, photos, and videos, and stay up-to-date with the latest trends and news from around the world.

Entertainment Apps: Enjoy your favorite music, movies, and TV shows with entertainment apps like Spotify, YouTube, Netflix, and Amazon Prime Video.

Stream music, watch videos, and discover new content to keep yourself entertained wherever you go.

Maps and Navigation: Navigate to your destination with ease using maps and navigation apps like Google Maps. Get real-time traffic updates, find nearby places of interest, and get turn-by-turn directions to reach your destination efficiently.

File Manager: Manage your files and documents with the built-in file manager app. Browse, organize, and transfer files between your device storage, microSD card, and cloud storage services like Google Drive and Samsung Cloud.

Health and Fitness: Keep track of your health and fitness goals with apps like Samsung Health. Monitor your activity levels, track your workouts, and maintain a healthy lifestyle with features such as step tracking, heart rate monitoring, and calorie tracking.

Device Maintenance: Ensure optimal performance and efficiency with the device maintenance app. Monitor battery usage, optimize device storage, and scan for malware and security threats to keep your device running smoothly.

These are just a few of the essential apps and features available on your Samsung Galaxy S24+. Explore the Galaxy Store and Google Play Store to discover even more apps and customize your device to suit your preferences and lifestyle.

4.1. Camera Functions And Tips

The camera on your Samsung Galaxy S24+ is a powerful tool for capturing stunning photos and videos. Familiarize yourself with its functions and follow these tips to take your photography to the next level:

CAMERA MODES

Auto Mode: Perfect for everyday photography, Auto mode automatically adjusts settings for optimal results in various lighting conditions.

Pro Mode: Take full control of settings like ISO, shutter speed, and white balance to customize your shot and achieve professional-quality results.

Night Mode: Capture clear and detailed photos in low-light environments by utilizing Night mode, which enhances brightness and reduces noise.

Portrait Mode: Create beautifully blurred backgrounds to make your subject stand out using Portrait mode, ideal for portraits and close-up shots.

Panorama Mode: Capture sweeping landscapes and wide scenes with Panorama mode, which stitches multiple images together seamlessly.

Food Mode: Make your food photos look mouthwatering with Food mode, which enhances colors and textures for appetizing shots.

Pro Video Mode: Record videos with manual control over settings like exposure, focus, and audio levels, allowing for professional-grade video capture.

CAMERA SETTINGS

Experiment with different camera settings to customize your shooting experience. Adjust options such as aspect ratio, grid lines, timer, and image stabilization to suit your preferences.
Enable features like HDR (High Dynamic Range) to capture well-balanced photos with enhanced detail in both shadows and highlights.

FOCUS AND COMPOSITION

Tap on the screen to focus on a specific subject before taking a photo. You can also adjust the focus and

exposure by sliding your finger up or down on the
screen.

Pay attention to composition principles such as the rule
of thirds, leading lines, and symmetry to create visually
appealing photos.

USE OF LIGHTING

Take advantage of natural light whenever possible, as it
produces the most flattering results. Position your
subject facing the light source for even illumination.
Experiment with different lighting conditions, such as
backlighting and side lighting, to add depth and drama to
your photos.

EDITING AND FILTERS

Enhance your photos with built-in editing tools and
filters. Adjust parameters like brightness, contrast, and
saturation to fine-tune your images.

Experiment with various filters and effects to add a creative touch to your photos, but use them sparingly to avoid over-processing.

STEADY SHOOTING

Keep your hands steady while taking photos to avoid blurriness. If necessary, use a tripod or stabilize your arms against a solid surface for sharper images.
Enable features like Optical Image Stabilization (OIS) and Super Steady mode to minimize camera shake and capture smoother videos.
By mastering the functions of your Galaxy S24+'s camera and implementing these tips, you can unleash your creativity and capture stunning photos and videos in any situation. Don't hesitate to experiment and explore new techniques to elevate your photography skills further.

4.2. Messaging and Calling

Messaging and calling are fundamental features of your Samsung Galaxy S24+, enabling seamless communication with friends, family, and colleagues. Here's how to make the most of these essential functions:

MESSAGING APPS

Messages: The Messages app allows you to send and receive text messages (SMS) and multimedia messages (MMS). You can also engage in group chats, share photos, videos, and audio messages, and use stickers and emojis to express yourself.

Chat Apps: Explore messaging apps like WhatsApp, Facebook Messenger, and Telegram for additional messaging features such as end-to-end encryption, voice and video calls, and multimedia sharing.

CALLING

Phone: The Phone app is your go-to for making and receiving voice calls. Dial a number directly, access your contacts list, or use speed dial for quick calling. You can also view call history, set up voicemail, and block unwanted callers.

Video Calls: Make face-to-face calls with video calling apps like Google Duo, Skype, and WhatsApp. Enjoy high-quality video calls with friends and family, whether they're across the street or around the world.

VoIP Calling: Explore Voice over Internet Protocol (VoIP) calling services like Skype, WhatsApp, and Google Voice for cost-effective calling over Wi-Fi or mobile data. VoIP calls can be an excellent option for international calls or when traveling abroad to avoid roaming charges.

ADVANCED CALLING FEATURES

HD Voice: Enjoy crystal-clear voice quality with HD Voice, which provides enhanced audio for calls made between compatible devices.

Wi-Fi Calling: Stay connected even in areas with poor cellular reception by enabling Wi-Fi Calling. This feature allows you to make and receive calls over a Wi-Fi network.

Call Screening and Blocking: Use call screening and blocking features to filter out unwanted calls and spam. You can block specific numbers, enable call screening to identify unknown callers, and use call blocking apps for additional protection.

MESSAGING AND CALLING SETTINGS

Customize messaging and calling settings to suit your preferences. Adjust options such as notification sounds, vibration patterns, and call forwarding settings to personalize your communication experience.

Explore additional features like Do Not Disturb mode, which silences calls and notifications during specified times, and driving mode, which provides hands-free calling and messaging while driving.

Whether you're sending a quick text message, making a phone call, or engaging in a video chat, your Samsung Galaxy S24+ offers a variety of messaging and calling options to keep you connected with the people who matter most. Experiment with different apps and features to find the communication methods that best suit your needs and lifestyle.

4.3. Email and Productivity Apps

Efficient email management and productivity are crucial for staying organized and maximizing your Samsung Galaxy S24+ usage. Here's how to utilize email and productivity apps effectively:

EMAIL APPS

Samsung Email: The Samsung Email app provides a robust email management solution with support for various email providers, including Gmail, Outlook, Yahoo, and more. Use it to access multiple email accounts, compose and send emails, and organize your inbox with folders and filters.

Gmail: If you use Gmail, the Gmail app offers a seamless email experience with features such as categorized inbox tabs, smart replies, and priority notifications. Stay productive with powerful search capabilities and customizable email organization.

Third-Party Email Apps: Explore third-party email apps like Microsoft Outlook, BlueMail, and Edison Mail for additional features such as email scheduling, customizable swipe actions, and integrated calendar functionality.

Productivity Apps

Calendar: Stay organized and manage your schedule with the Calendar app. Create events, set reminders, and sync your appointments across devices to stay on track with your commitments.

Tasks and To-Do Lists: Keep track of tasks and to-do lists with apps like Google Tasks, Microsoft To Do, or Any.do. Organize tasks by priority, due date, or category, and set reminders to ensure you stay focused and productive.

Notes and Document Editors: Capture ideas, jot down notes, and collaborate on documents with apps like Samsung Notes, Google Keep, or Microsoft Office apps. Create, edit, and share documents, *spreadsheets, and presentations on the go.*

File Management: Manage your files and documents with apps like Google Drive, Microsoft OneDrive, or

Samsung's My Files app. Store, organize, and access your files from anywhere, and easily share them with others.

Cloud Storage: Take advantage of cloud storage services like Dropbox, iCloud, or Samsung Cloud to back up your important files, photos, and documents securely. Access your files from any device and share them with others seamlessly.

Integration and Syncing: Ensure seamless integration and syncing between email and productivity apps by connecting them to your preferred accounts and services. Sync calendars, tasks, and documents across devices to stay productive whether you're on your Galaxy S24+, computer, or tablet.

Customization and Settings: Customize email and productivity app settings to suit your preferences and workflow. Adjust notification settings, email signatures, and default calendar views to optimize your productivity experience.

Explore advanced features like email aliases, automatic email sorting, and email templates to streamline your email management process and boost efficiency.

By leveraging email and productivity apps effectively on your Samsung Galaxy S24+, you can streamline communication, stay organized, and maximize your productivity wherever you go. Experiment with different apps and features to find the combination that works best for your workflow and lifestyle.

4.4. Exploring Samsung Services

Samsung offers a range of services designed to enhance your experience with your Galaxy S24+ and other Samsung devices. Here's an overview of some key Samsung services to explore:

Samsung Account

A Samsung Account provides access to a variety of services and features, including Samsung Cloud storage, Galaxy Store apps, and device customization options. Sign up for a Samsung Account on your Galaxy S24+ to enjoy benefits such as seamless device backup and restore, cross-device synchronization, and exclusive offers and promotions.

Samsung Cloud

Samsung Cloud offers secure cloud storage for your photos, videos, documents, and other important data. Backup your Galaxy S24+ automatically to Samsung Cloud to safeguard your files and ensure they're always accessible.

Sync your data across multiple Samsung devices, including smartphones, tablets, and wearables, for seamless access to your files wherever you go.

Galaxy Store

The Galaxy Store is Samsung's official app store, offering a wide selection of apps, games, themes, and customization options for your Galaxy S24+.
Explore a curated collection of apps optimized for Samsung devices, including exclusive titles and deals available only to Galaxy device users.

Samsung Pay

Samsung Pay is a convenient and secure mobile payment service that allows you to make contactless payments using your Galaxy S24+. Add your credit, debit, and loyalty cards to Samsung Pay to make payments in-store, online, and in-app with ease.
Take advantage of features like Samsung Rewards, which allows you to earn points for every transaction and redeem them for rewards, discounts, and special offers.

Samsung Health

Samsung Health is a comprehensive health and fitness platform that helps you track your activity, monitor your wellness goals, and stay motivated to live a healthier lifestyle.
Use Samsung Health to track your steps, exercise, sleep patterns, and nutrition, and access personalized insights and recommendations to improve your overall well-being.

Bixby

Bixby is Samsung's virtual assistant, designed to help you get things done more efficiently using voice commands and AI technology.
Use Bixby to control your device, search for information, set reminders, send messages, and perform tasks hands-free, all with simple voice commands.

Samsung Members

Samsung Members is a community and support platform that provides access to tips, tutorials, troubleshooting guides, and customer support services.

Connect with other Samsung users, participate in discussions, and get help with your Galaxy S24+ from Samsung experts and community members.

Exploring and utilizing Samsung services can enhance your Galaxy S24+ experience and unlock additional features and capabilities. Take advantage of these services to personalize your device, stay connected, and make the most of your Samsung ecosystem.

CHAPTER 5

CUSTOMIZATION OPTIONS

There are a ton of customization choices available on the Samsung Galaxy S24+ to help you personalize and customize your device. How to customize your Galaxy S24+ is as follows:

Customizing the Home Screen

Rearrange the folders, widgets, and app icons to personalize your Home screen. To access settings for adding widgets, modifying wallpapers, and tweaking screen grid layouts, long-press on an empty section of the Home screen.

Wallpapers and Themes

To alter the look and feel of your device, pick from a number of pre-installed themes or download more from the Galaxy Themes app. Personalize system sounds, icons, and wallpapers to reflect your personal style. Use dynamic wallpapers, live wallpapers, or custom photo wallpapers to make your lock screen uniquely yours. Additionally, you may turn on Always On Display to see helpful data and designs even while your phone is locked.

Styles and Packs of Icons

Use third-party icon packs that you may get from the Galaxy Store or other app stores to personalize the icons for your apps. Play around with various icon forms, colors, and styles to produce a unified and eye-catching Home screen arrangement.

Edge Lighting and Edge Panels

Use Edge Panels to your advantage to rapidly access tools, programs, and shortcuts. Add your preferred contacts and apps to Edge Panels to enable quick access from any screen.

To provide visual notifications to incoming calls, messages, and other alerts, turn on Edge Lighting. To fit your tastes, select from a variety of colors and lighting effects.

Constantly Observable (AOD)

You may customize the Always On Display settings to show important details like the battery level, time, date, and alerts even when your device is sleeping. Customize your AOD experience with a variety of clock designs, widgets, and backgrounds.

Keyboard and Hand gestures

Choose between gesture-based and conventional navigation buttons to personalize your navigation options. To improve your navigation experience, change the gesture sensitivity, navigation bar arrangement, and full-screen gesture settings.

Security and Lock Screen

Add unique wallpapers, clock faces, and app shortcuts to make your lock screen uniquely yours. Personalize security settings, lock screen alerts, and biometric authentication techniques like face and fingerprint recognition to your liking.

Noises and Motions

To make your device's audio experience uniquely yours, adjust the vibration and sound settings. For calls, messages, and alerts, change the vibration intensity, ringtone, and notification sound. Make unique vibration patterns for particular connections or applications.

Display settings and fonts

Try experimenting with different font sizes and styles to personalize how text appears on your device. Optimize clarity and comfort of watching by adjusting display parameters like color balance, blue light filter, and screen resolution.

Advanced Configurations and Features

Explore more in-depth options and advanced features to fully personalize your Galaxy S24+ experience. Examine features such as gaming booster, multi-window mode, Bixby routines, and device maintenance to customize your smartphone according to your usage style and habits.

Your Samsung Galaxy S24+ can be customized with a multitude of choices to suit your own preferences and style. Take your time experimenting and exploring with various customization options to make your gadget feel like a real work of art.

5.1. Creating a Customized Home Screen

With the many customization choices available on the Samsung Galaxy S24+, you can make your Home screen uniquely your own and arrange things to suit your tastes and style. Here's how to personalize your Home screen:

Backgrounds

Whether it's a minimalist pattern, a beloved picture, or a picturesque scenery, pick a wallpaper that appeals to you. To access other wallpaper alternatives, navigate the Galaxy Themes app or long-press on an empty section of the Home screen, select "Wallpapers," and pick one of the pre-installed options.

Gadgets

You may quickly access information and functionality without launching programs by adding widgets to your Home screen. To access a range of widgets, including weather, calendar, clock, and music player widgets, long-press on an empty section of the Home screen, select "Widgets," and then make your selection.

Icons and Layout for Apps

Adapt the app icon layout to your own style choices. You may resize widgets to fit your preferred layout, create folders to put relevant apps together, and drag app icons around to reorganize them.

Try out several icon packs and styles that are accessible from outside sources to give your Home screen a new appearance. The device settings also allow you to change the sizes and forms of the icons.

Concepts

Using the Galaxy Themes app, you can alter the device's overall appearance and feel. With the extensive customization possibilities that themes provide, including wallpapers, icons, system colors, and sounds, you may put together a visually pleasing and unified Home screen configuration.

Motions and Abbreviations

Utilize shortcuts and gestures to expedite navigation and gain access to frequently used features and apps. Configure motions to launch certain apps straight from the Home screen, such as double-tapping to lock the screen or swiping.

Personalized Dock

Put your most-used apps in the Dock, which is located at the bottom of your Home screen, for convenient access. You can drag an app icon to the Dock area by long-pressing on it, or you can drag apps out of the Dock.

Notification Medals

To receive notifications about unread messages straight from your Home screen, turn on notification badges. Notification badges serve as visual signals on app icons, showing how many emails, missed calls, and unread messages there are.

Files and Arrangement

Using folders to bring related apps together can help you keep your Home screen neat and organized. To create a folder, drag and drop the icons of one program over another. Then, change the folder name and add other apps as needed. This lessens clutter and facilitates finding apps quickly.

Bar for Search and Widgets

Change the location, size, and look of the Search bar located at the top of your Home screen. Additionally, you may add search widgets to your Home screen to provide quick access to contacts, apps, online search, and more.

Wallpapers, widgets, themes, and custom layouts allow you to modify your Home screen to create a one-of-a-kind arrangement that expresses your style and improves your smartphone experience. Try out several customizing settings to get the ideal appearance for your Samsung Galaxy S24+.

5.2. Customizing Themes and Wallpaper

With the help of themes and wallpapers, you may express your preferences and personalize the appearance and feel of your Samsung Galaxy S24+. Here's how to alter your device's wallpaper and themes:

Concepts

With the Galaxy Themes app, Samsung provides a vast selection of themes that let you totally change how your smartphone looks.

To browse and download themes, open the Galaxy Themes app from your Home screen or app drawer. To locate themes that appeal to you, you can browse categories like Nature, Abstract, Minimalistic, and more. After selecting a theme you like, tap on it to see a preview and download it to your phone. To create a unified appearance, themes can alter the system colors, wallpaper, icons, and even the noises.

You may further personalize your themes by making changes to specific components like wallpapers, fonts, and icon packs. In the Theme Store, several themes additionally provide more customization choices.

Backgrounds

Custom wallpapers that represent your interests and personality might help you make your device uniquely yours.

To open the wallpaper selection menu, long-press on a blank space on the Home screen and choose "Wallpapers." The Galaxy Themes app offers pre-installed wallpapers that you may use, or you can use your own images as wallpapers.

Look through a variety of categories, including Art, Abstract, Landscapes, and more, to discover wallpapers

MASTERING YOUR SAMSUNG GALAXY S24+

that speak to you. To focus your search and reduce the number of results, use keyword specific searches.

After choosing a wallpaper, preview it and, if needed, crop it to fit your screen precisely. To set it as your wallpaper for your home screen, lock screen, or both, hit "Set as wallpaper."

Adaptive Lock Screen

Use the Dynamic Lock Screen function to have your lock screen wallpaper dynamically changed based on predefined categories, including travel, art, or landscapes.

Go to the Wallpaper options, enable Dynamic Lock Screen, and choose the categories you wish to add. Every time you open your device, the wallpaper on your lock screen will change on a regular basis to give it a new appearance.

Live Desktop Images

Live wallpapers that react to your touch and movements can give your Home screen an interactive touch.

To view and download animated wallpapers, navigate to the Wallpaper settings and look for the Live Wallpapers area. To add some life to your smartphone, select from a variety of dynamic images, including shifting landscapes, underwater views, and geometric patterns.

Planned Wallpaper Updates

Scheduled wallpaper changes that automatically cycle through a collection of wallpapers will keep your smartphone looking new.

In the Wallpaper options, enable Scheduled Wallpaper Changes and select the wallpaper source and frequency. The pre-installed wallpapers, the Gallery, and the Dynamic Lock Screen are the options for rotating wallpapers.

You can genuinely customize your Samsung Galaxy S24+ with themes and wallpaper choices. Try out various themes, wallpapers, and configurations to make your gadget a one-of-a-kind, eye-catching visual representation of your taste and individuality.

5.3. Preferences for Sound and Display

You may personalize your Samsung Galaxy S24+ to suit your tastes and improve the way it works by adjusting the sound and display settings. Here's how to change these configurations:

Sound Preferences

Ringtone and Notification Sounds: Choose your favorite ringtone and notification sounds to personalize the sound profile of your device. You can add your own unique sounds or select from the pre-installed tones.

Volume Settings: Change the loudness of the following audio categories: System, Media, Notifications, and Ringtone. You can rapidly modify the volume levels on your smartphone by using the volume controls on the side, or you can access the extensive volume settings in the Sound settings menu.

Personalized vibration patterns can be set for touch feedback, calls, and notifications. Adapt the vibration patterns and intensities to your own tastes.

To mute incoming calls, notifications, and alarms during designated hours, enable the Do Not Disturb mode. Make changes to the Do Not Disturb settings so that specific contacts or apps can have an exception.

SHOW PREFERENCES

Brightness and Adaptive Brightness: You can manually change the screen's brightness or turn on Adaptive Brightness, which automatically modifies the brightness according to the surrounding lighting. Adjust the Adaptive Brightness settings to your preferred brightness levels.

Blue Light Filter: By turning down the blue light emissions from the screen, you can lessen eye strain and get a better night's sleep. You may program the Blue Light Filter to turn on automatically at night.

Screen Timeout: You can adjust the screen timeout duration to determine how long your device will remain active before shutting down automatically. Pick from a variety of timeout durations, from 15 seconds to 10 minutes, or choose "Stay awake" to leave the screen on forever.

Screen Mode: To change the saturation and color balance of your image, select from a variety of screen settings, including Vivid, Natural, and Basic. Adjust the screen mode settings to get the correct color saturation and accuracy.

Screen Resolution: To improve display quality or prolong battery life, change the screen resolution. Depending on your needs and tastes, select from resolution options like HD+, FHD+, or WQHD+.

Font and Display Size: To increase readability and accessibility, change the font's style and size. To change the size of text and interface elements, select a font style and modify the display size settings.

On your Samsung Galaxy S24+, you may personalize the user experience to fit your tastes and improve usability by adjusting the sound and display settings. Try out various configurations to determine which one best suits your requirements and tastes.

CHAPTER 6

ADVANCED SETTINGS

Investigate the advanced settings of your Samsung Galaxy S24+ to realize all of its potential. You may personalize and optimize your smartphone using these settings to create a more effective and efficient user experience. Take a look at these important advanced settings:

Developer Choices

Tap the Build number many times in the About phone section of the Settings menu to unlock Developer Options. Power users can access debugging tools and additional functionality using Developer Options. Developer Options contains settings for background programs, system animations, USB debugging, and other things. When adjusting settings under Developer

Options, be cautious because some may have an impact on the stability and performance of your device.

Configuring Accessibility

Examine the accessibility settings on your device to make it suitable for users with particular requirements or tastes. To increase accessibility and usefulness, make necessary adjustments to the vision, hearing, dexterity, and interaction settings.

Users with disabilities or limits can benefit from extra assistance through features like Voice Assistant, Magnifier Window, and Accessibility shortcuts.

Enhancer for Games

Game Booster, a tool that enhances device performance for gaming, will improve your gaming experience. When you play, Game Booster automatically modifies the settings to maximize gaming performance and reduce distractions.

To enable features like Screen Touch Lock, Game Launcher, and Performance Mode for more fluid gameplay and better graphics, adjust the Game Booster settings.

Security and Biometric Configurations

Tailor the biometric authentication configurations to improve privacy and security on your device. Configure features for safe unlocking and authentication, such as Face, Fingerprint, and Iris recognition.

Investigate extra security options like Samsung Knox, Find My Mobile, and Secure Folder to preserve your data and defend your smartphone from unwanted access.

Power Saving and Batteries

Utilize power-saving technologies and smart battery settings to maximize battery life and performance. To extend battery life and lower power consumption, adjust settings like Power Mode, Adaptive Battery, and Battery Usage.

To reduce battery drain and increase uptime, make use of features like Background Restrictions, App Power Monitor, and Adaptive Power Saving.

Memory and Storage Management

Utilize advanced options for memory usage and storage optimization to efficiently manage storage and memory. To increase performance, preserve device health, and free up space, make use of features like Smart Storage, Clear Cache, and Device Care.

To manage files, programs, and data storage locations, such as internal storage, microSD cards, and cloud storage services, explore the storage settings.

Updating and maintaining the system

Update your device with the most recent security patches and software upgrades. In the Software Update area of the Settings menu, you can either manually check for updates or enable automatic system updates.

Use the Device Care tool to carry out routine maintenance activities like storage cleansing, security scans, and device optimization. To guarantee optimum performance, keep an eye on the device's performance, battery life, and storage capacity.

You can enhance performance, access new features, and personalize your Samsung Galaxy S24+ to fit your tastes and usage patterns by exploring the advanced options. To make the most of your device's capabilities and improve your overall experience, spend some time experimenting with these options.

6.1. Features for Security and Privacy

It is crucial to safeguard your private information and make sure your Samsung Galaxy S24+ is secure. Examine the different privacy and security settings on your smartphone to protect your data and keep your mind at ease:

Options for Screen Locking

To stop unwanted access to your smartphone, set up screen lock options like PIN, pattern, password, fingerprint recognition, or facial recognition. Select a safe locking technique and personalize extra security features like lock screen alerts and Smart Lock settings.

Safe Folder

Your device's Secure Folder offers a private, encrypted storage area for private documents, images, apps, and other data. To safeguard private data, use a secure folder and store it somewhere other than on your device. For an extra degree of protection, you can configure Secure Folder using a PIN, pattern, password, or biometric verification.

Locate My Cell Phone

A strong security feature called Find My Mobile assists you in finding, locking, and remotely wiping your device in the event that it is lost or stolen. Turn on Find My Mobile from the Settings menu, then use the Find My Mobile website or app to set up remote controls to ring, locate, or delete data from your device.

Verification through Biometrics

To unlock your device quickly and securely, make use of biometric identification techniques like face recognition, fingerprint recognition, and iris scanning. To unlock your device, access the Secure Folder, and securely authenticate transactions, register your biometric data in the Biometrics and Security settings.

Permissions for the App

Control which apps have access to private information and functionality on your device by managing app permissions. To make sure that apps are only able to access the data they require to operate correctly, go through and alter the app permissions under the App Permissions settings.

Configuring Privacy:

By changing the settings for data sharing, location tracking, and targeted advertising, you can safeguard your privacy. To manage the way that applications and services gather, utilize, and share your data, go through and adjust the privacy settings found in the Privacy menu.

Safe VPN and Wi-Fi

With features like Virtual Private Network (VPN) and Secure Wi-Fi, you can safeguard your online privacy and stay safe when using public Wi-Fi networks. When connected to unprotected networks, use Secure Wi-Fi to automatically encrypt your internet connection. To browse the internet safely and anonymously, encrypt your traffic and set up a virtual private network (VPN).

Safe Folder Lock and App Lock

App Lock and Secure Folder Lock allow you to secure certain apps or the whole Secure Folder. By demanding authentication before granting access, you may use these capabilities to give sensitive apps and data an additional degree of protection.

Frequent updates for software

To guard against any vulnerabilities and security threats, keep your device up to speed with the most recent software updates and security patches. To keep your device safe and secure, turn on automatic software updates in the Software Update settings or manually check for updates.

You can secure your private data, prevent unwanted access to your device, and keep control over your privacy settings by making use of the security and privacy features on your Samsung Galaxy S24+. By taking proactive measures to secure your device, you can rest easy knowing that your data is secure.

6.2. Upkeep and Enhancement of Devices

Maintaining and optimizing your Samsung Galaxy S24+ on a regular basis is crucial to keeping it operating smoothly. To guarantee optimum performance and lifetime, investigate the device maintenance and optimization capabilities available on your device:

Device Maintenance

A built-in feature called Device Care offers extensive capabilities for optimizing and maintaining devices. To keep an eye on your device's performance, battery life, storage space, and security status, navigate to Device Care from the Settings menu.

To optimize device performance, clean out unwanted files and cache data, scan for malware and security concerns, and control battery consumption to maximize uptime, use Device Care.

Optimizing Batteries

Use battery optimization options to extend battery life and reduce power consumption. To see battery usage data, find apps that use a lot of power, and activate power-saving features like Power Saving Mode and Adaptive Battery, go to the Battery settings.

Utilize cutting-edge energy optimization features to reduce power drain and increase battery life throughout the day, such as Adaptive Power Saving and Background Restrictions.

Storage Administration

Effective storage management will preserve device performance and free up space. To recover storage space, utilize the Storage options to analyze storage utilization by category, find large files and unused apps, and remove superfluous files and cache.

To automate storage cleanup chores and maintain the smooth operation of your device, investigate storage optimization technologies like Smart Storage and Auto Optimization.

Optimizing Performance

Use performance optimization features to maximize the responsiveness and performance of your device. Utilize the Performance options to keep an eye on memory, CPU, and app performance as well as to identify any apps that might be interfering with functionality.

To maximize app speed, free up memory, and enhance overall device responsiveness, make use of performance optimization tools like App Optimization and Memory Management.

Device Safety

Make sure your device has strong security features to protect it from security threats and vulnerabilities. To secure your smartphone, data, and privacy, turn on security features like Samsung Knox, Secure Startup, and Find My Mobile.

Enable automatic software updates in the Software Update settings to stay up to speed on security updates and patches. Make sure the most recent security fixes are updated on your device by manually checking for updates on a regular basis.

Continual Upkeep

Include routine device maintenance in your routine to maintain the optimal performance of your Samsung Galaxy S24+. To guarantee optimum device performance and dependability, carry out routinely checking for software updates, deleting cache data, and improving app performance.

To simplify device maintenance and maintain optimal performance, set up automated maintenance activities and reminders using technologies like Auto Optimization and Scheduled Maintenance.

You can make sure that your Samsung Galaxy S24+ stays safe, responsive, and efficient over time by implementing routine device maintenance and optimization procedures. For a seamless and pleasurable user experience, take proactive measures to optimize speed, manage storage efficiently, and safeguard your device against security threats.

6.3. Features for Accessibility

The Samsung Galaxy S24+ has a number of accessibility features that are intended to improve the device's usability for people with special needs or disabilities. Examine these functions to improve usability and accessibility:

VISION

Turn on Vision Assistant to gain access to a variety of accessible features designed with users with visual impairments in mind. To enhance visibility and readability, features including a screen reader, magnifier, high contrast, and color modification options are available.

Magnifier Window: To make content on the screen easier to see, use the Magnifier Window feature. Use simple motions to navigate through magnified content and adjust the magnification levels.

Font and Display Size: To make text and interface components larger and easier to read, adjust the font size, style, and display size settings. Modify the font scale and screen zoom settings to suit personal tastes.
Turn on Dark Mode to lessen eye strain and enhance sight in dimly lit areas. To make system applications and interfaces easier on the eyes, Dark Mode applies a dark color scheme to them.

Listening

To enhance audio accessibility for individuals with hearing problems, utilize the hearing assistant functions. To improve music clarity and quality, features like mono audio, adjustable audio balance settings, and a sound amplifier are included.

With Live Transcribe, you can instantly translate spoken words into text and create subtitles for talks, seminars, and other audio recordings. To fit your tastes, change the language, color, and font size.

Mobility

Customize the interaction control settings to make it easier for users with mobility impairments to navigate and control your device. To make typical chores easier to complete, utilize features like gesture control, assistant menu, and single tap mode.

Turn on the Assistant Menu to have easy access to shortcuts and important functions from anywhere on the screen. Assistant Menu offers a floating menu with customized gestures, accessibility features, and navigation shortcuts.

Thinking and Education

Explore accessibility options designed with persons with learning and cognitive disabilities in mind. Usability is increased and device operation is made simpler with features including voice commands, interaction prompts, and a reduced interface.

Voice Assistant: You can use voice commands to operate your device by using Voice Assistant. Voice Assistant uses natural language instructions to navigate menus, apps, and settings while providing spoken feedback and assistance.

EXTRA FEATURES FOR ACCESSIBILITY

One-Handed Mode: To make using the screen with one hand easier, enable One-Handed Mode. You can use a gesture shortcut or swipe down from the bottom corner of the screen to enter one-handed mode.

Direct Access: You can easily activate accessibility features with a triple-click of the Home button by customizing the Direct Access settings. For easier access, assign shortcuts to functions like the screen reader, magnifier, and accessibility settings.

You may increase accessibility, boost usability, and make the Samsung Galaxy S24+ more inclusive for people with a range of needs and abilities by taking advantage of the accessibility features on the device. Examine these options to personalize your gadget and enhance its usability and accessibility.

CHAPTER 7

TROUBLESHOOTING AND MAINTENANCE

It can be annoying to come into problems with your Samsung Galaxy S24+, but you can keep it functioning properly by knowing how to solve common issues and doing routine maintenance. This is a how-to for maintaining and debugging your Galaxy S24+:

Reboot or Restart

Try resetting your smartphone if you're having minor problems like slow performance or unresponsive apps. Frequently, short-term issues can be fixed with a quick restart, returning functioning to normal.

Empty the Cache and Data

Caches and data for individual apps can be cleared to help fix problems like freezing, crashing, or using too much storage. Navigate to Settings > Applications, pick the offending app, and then make the necessary selections to delete any cache or data.

Upgrade the software

Make sure the software on your device is up to date by applying any updates that are available. To manually check for updates or, for convenience, to activate automatic updates, go to Settings > Software update > Download and install.

Examine your memory and storage

App crashes and performance problems might be caused by low memory or storage capacity. By eliminating files or programs that aren't needed, you may clear up space on your device and monitor its storage and memory utilization by going to Settings > Device care > Storage and Memory.

Maximize Battery Consumption

By modifying battery settings and turning on power-saving modes, you may extend battery life and maximize power consumption. To reduce power drain and increase battery life, make use of features like Adaptive power, Power Saving Mode, and Background Restrictions.

Reset Configuration

Think about returning your gadget to its factory default settings if you're having trouble with it staying stable or performing poorly. To reset network, display, sound, and other settings without erasing personal information, go to Settings > General management > Reset > Reset settings.

Safe Mode

Put your smartphone in Safe Mode to solve problems brought on by unofficial apps. Because only pre-installed programs can operate in Safe Mode, it is simpler to find and remove troublesome apps that might be the source of problems.

Factory Reset

Try a factory reset as a last option to get your device back to how it was intended to be. Since this procedure will remove all data and settings from your device, make a backup of your data before beginning. To execute a factory reset, navigate to Settings > General management > Reset > Factory data reset.

Speak with Support

Do not hesitate to call Samsung support or visit an authorized service center for assistance if you are unable to address a problem on your own. For assistance and direction in diagnosing and resolving more complicated difficulties, contact Samsung's support staff.

These troubleshooting and maintenance instructions can help you fix common problems, maximize performance, and maintain the smooth operation of your Samsung Galaxy S24+. Maintaining your gadget with proactive troubleshooting and routine maintenance can help guarantee a smooth and pleasurable user experience.

7.1. Typical Problems and Their Fixes

It can be annoying to run into problems with your Samsung Galaxy S24+, but there are easy fixes for a lot of common issues. The following are some typical problems with your device and how to fix them:

Fast Battery Drain

The fix is to go to Settings > Battery > Battery consumption and look for any apps that are using too much battery life. To reduce battery drain, turn on power-saving modes like Power Saving Mode or Adaptive Battery, close background apps, and change settings.

Overheating Of The Device

Solution: Steer clear of placing your gadget in the sun or extreme heat for long periods of time. Before using your device again, make sure all extra accessories are removed, resource-intensive programs are closed, and the device has had time to cool.

The App Freezes Or Crashes

Solution: Go to Settings > Applications > [App Name] > Storage > and delete the app's cache and data. Clear data and/or cache. Get the most recent version of the software from the Samsung Galaxy Store or Google Play Store.

Sluggish Performance

Restarting your device will remove temporary files and update system processes. To clear the cache partition, choose "Wipe cache partition" after booting into recovery mode (hold the Volume Up and Power buttons).

Problems with Bluetooth or Wi-Fi Connectivity:

Solution: Disable Bluetooth and Wi-Fi and then enable them again. Re-add the Bluetooth device or Wi-Fi network after forgetting it. Go to Settings > General management > Reset > Reset network settings to update the software on your smartphone and reset the network configuration.

Unsatisfactory Call Quality

Solution: Check to make sure the speakers and microphone on your device aren't broken or blocked. If available, turn on VoLTE (Voice over LTE) and disable Wi-Fi calling. Verify local network coverage and carrier updates.

Issues with Screen Sensitivity

Solution: Wipe off the screen and take off any cases or screen protectors that could impede touch sensitivity. Go to Settings > Display > Touch sensitivity to change the touch sensitivity settings.

Camera Not Performing Correctly

Restart your smartphone and make sure there are no impurities or dirt particles on the camera lens. Go to Settings > Apps > Camera > Storage > Clear cache/Clear data to remove the cache and data associated with the camera app. Update the software on your device and the camera app.

Problems with GPS or location

Solution: Go to Settings > Biometrics and security > Location and enable location services. Make sure the software or apps requiring GPS have location permissions enabled. Go to Settings > General management > Reset > to reset the location settings. Reset the location's parameters.

Touchscreen Not answering

Solution: Wipe the screen clean and take off any cases or screen protectors that could obstruct touchscreen operation. When the device restarts, see whether there is a software update available.
Try getting in touch with Samsung support or going to an approved service center if you're still having problems

with your Samsung Galaxy S24+. If necessary, they can set up repairs or offer more troubleshooting instructions.

7.2. Upgrades and Updates for Software

For best performance, security, and access to new features, make sure your Samsung Galaxy S24+ is running the most recent software updates and upgrades. What you should know about your device's software upgrades and updates is as follows:

Frequent Updates For Software

Samsung regularly upgrades its software to fix faults, boost efficiency, and strengthen security. These upgrades might provide new features, enhanced system stability, and battery life and performance optimizations.
To guarantee that your device gets updates as soon as they are made available, turn on automatic software updates in the Settings menu. Navigate to Settings >

Software update > Install and download. To enable automatic updates, enable auto download over Wi-Fi.

Manually Searching for Updates

If you want to install updates right away or if you don't want automatic updates, you can manually check for software updates. Navigate to Settings > Software update > Install and download. To manually search for updates that are available, check for updates.
In the event that an update is available, download and install it by following the on-screen instructions. Make sure your smartphone has enough battery life and is linked to a reliable Wi-Fi network before starting the upgrade process.

Patches For Security

Samsung releases monthly security patches to fix vulnerabilities and shield your device from security threats in addition to significant software updates. The integrity and security of your device depend on these security patches.

Generally, Samsung distributes security fixes through over-the-air updates, which are sent to your device automatically or that you can manually verify and apply via the Settings menu.

Significant Software Updates

Samsung periodically delivers large software updates that bring about notable modifications and new functionality to your device, such as Android version updates. Along with performance advancements and compatibility with new apps and services, these upgrades might also feature UI improvements.

Samsung usually notifies customers of major software updates ahead of time and prompts eligible devices to download and install the update. For an easy upgrading process, keep a watch out for announcements and adhere to Samsung's recommendations.

Getting Ready for Updates

It's crucial to back up your data before installing software updates or upgrades to avoid losing it in the event that there are any unanticipated problems with the update process. Make a backup of your contacts, images, movies, and other crucial data to an external drive, Google Drive, or Samsung Cloud.

To avoid disruptions during the update process, make sure your device is powered on or has enough battery life left. Before starting a software update, it's also advised to update your apps to the most recent versions available from the Google Play Store.

You can keep your Samsung Galaxy S24+ safe, dependable, and loaded with the newest features and enhancements by keeping up with software updates and upgrades. To keep your gadget operating efficiently, make it a practice to check for updates on a regular basis and install them right away.

7.3. Creating a Device Backup and Restore

Protecting your data and making sure you can quickly restore it in the event of loss, damage, or device replacement require backing up your Samsung Galaxy S24+. Here's how to successfully backup and restore your device:

CREATING A DEVICE BACKUP

Samsung Cloud Backup

The data on your device, including contacts, calendar entries, pictures, videos, apps, and settings, can be easily backed up with Samsung Cloud.
Go to Settings > Accounts and backup > Backup and restore > Back up data to begin backing up your smartphone to Samsung Cloud. To start the backup process, choose the data types you wish to backup and adhere to the on-screen directions.

Backup Google Account

Additionally, you can set up automatic backups for contacts, calendar events, app data, and settings using your Google account.
Navigate to Settings > Accounts and backup > Backup and restore > Google account backup to enable the feature. Toggle the switch to backup mode and choose the kinds of data you wish to store in backup.

Backup External Storage

Your files, pictures, videos, and other material can be manually backed up to external storage devices like USB drives, external hard drives, or microSD cards.
Using a compatible cable or adapter, connect the external storage device to your device. Then, copy and transfer files to the external storage device using the built-in file manager or an external file manager program.

Samsung Smart Switch

With the help of the flexible Samsung Smart Switch, you may backup your smartphone's data to an external storage device, a computer, or another device.
Using a USB cable, Wi-Fi connection, or external storage device, back up your data by following the on-screen instructions after downloading and installing the Samsung Smart Switch software on your computer or another Samsung device.

RESTORING YOUR ELECTRONIC EQUIPMENT:

Samsung Cloud Backup

Go to Settings > Accounts and backup > Backup and restore > Restore data to recover your smartphone from a Samsung Cloud backup. To begin the restoration process, choose the backup file you wish to restore from and adhere to the on-screen directions.

Restore Google Account

You have the option to recover your data from your Google account backup during the initial setup process when setting up a new device or after doing a factory reset.

When asked to log in to your Google account during setup, choose to restore data from an earlier device. To finish the repair process, adhere to the on-screen directions.

Restore Samsung Smart Switch

To restore your device from a backup kept on a computer, another device, or an external storage device, use Samsung Smart Switch.

To begin the restoration process, connect your device to a computer or another Samsung Smart Switch-running device, choose the backup file you wish to restore from, and then follow the on-screen directions.

Regularly backing up your Samsung Galaxy S24+ and being able to restore it from a backup can help you safeguard your important data, make moving devices easier, and recover from unplanned data loss. Develop the practice of routinely backing up your device to reduce the possibility of losing crucial data.

CHAPTER 8

TIPS AND TRICKS FOR YOUR SAMSUNG GALAXY S24+

With these pointers and techniques, you can maximize the capabilities of your Samsung Galaxy S24+ and improve your overall user experience:

Personalize Your Fast Settings

To reorganize or add shortcuts for your commonly used settings, long-press on the Quick Settings tiles. Tailor the layout so that you can quickly access key functions with a single swipe.

For Fast Access, Make Use of Edge Panels

To access tools, apps, and shortcuts with a swipe from the edge of the screen, enable Edge Panels under

118

Settings > Display > Edge screen. Organize Edge Panels with your preferred tasks, contacts, and apps for easy access.

Use Split Screen Multitasking to Your Advantage

To run two apps side by side at the same time, use split screen mode. To utilize the second app in split screen mode, launch the first app, then slide up from the bottom of the screen to reveal the Recent Apps menu.

Turn on the one-handed mode

Turn on One-Handed Mode to make using your device easier with one hand. To enable One-Handed Mode for a reduced screen size, swipe diagonally from the bottom corner of the screen or downward on the Home button.

Apply Voice Commands for Bixby

Utilize Bixby voice commands to operate your gadget without using your hands. Saying "Hey Bixby" or tapping the Bixby button will activate Bixby. You can then use voice commands to carry out tasks, look up information, or launch apps.
Enhance Device Care to Maximize Device Performance:

Utilize Device Care frequently to monitor battery life, maximize device performance, and free up storage. Maintain your smartphone by performing maintenance chores including app optimization, cache data clearing, and virus scanning.

Create Personalized Always On Display (AOD)

Customize the notification settings, background image, and clock styles on your device's Always On Display. To personalize your AOD experience, navigate to Settings >

Lock screen > Always On Display to access the AOD settings.

For Privacy, Use A Secure Folder

Use Secure Folder, a hidden, encrypted area on your device, to protect your private and confidential apps, pictures, and files. For more privacy and security, save sensitive data on a different device from what you normally use for regular storage.

Investigate Camera Features and Modes

Utilize the sophisticated camera settings and functions that come with your Galaxy S24+. Try out the manual control of the Pro mode, the low-light shooting of the Night mode, and the multi-shot option that allows you to take numerous pictures with a single click of the shutter.

Organize Yourself Using Samsung Notes

With Samsung Notes, you can easily scribble doodles, make lists, and record ideas. Using Samsung Cloud or other cloud storage services, you may sync your notes across devices and access them from any location.

Turn Navigation Gestures to Your Own

To improve the intuitiveness of using your device, customize the navigation gestures. Navigate to Settings > Display > Navigation bar > Navigation gestures and enable movements such as slide down for notifications, swipe up for Home, and swipe back to access previous information.

You may maximize the features and capabilities of your Samsung Galaxy S24+, personalize it, and streamline your workflow by implementing these tips and techniques into your everyday usage. Try out various features and settings to find new ways to improve your user experience.

8.1. Unknown Functions & Quick Links for Your Samsung Galaxy S24+

Discover shortcuts and hidden features to get the most out of your Samsung Galaxy S24+. Take a look at these lesser-known functions and quick cuts:

Shortcut for Quickly Launching the Camera

Even with the device locked, you may quickly access the camera by double-pressing the Power button. Take pictures of impromptu moments without opening your phone.

Tool for Smart Selection

For accurate screenshot capturing, use the Smart Select tool. To use Smart Select, press and hold the S Pen button while swiping over the screen. From there, you may trim, extract text, or make GIFs from the area you've picked.

123

Direct Message and Direct Dial

For your most trusted contacts, create shortcuts for direct dial and direct message. To add a shortcut from your home screen to a contact's phone number or message thread, long-press the Phone or Messages app icon and choose the contact.

A Game Launcher to Promote Better Gaming

Utilize Game Launcher to enhance your gaming experience. When playing a game, you can swipe up from the bottom of the screen to access Game Launcher, or you can tap the icon. To improve your gaming experience, you can record games, change the game's settings, and access extra features.

Safe Folder Hidden Applications

Use a Secure Folder to conceal important apps for an extra degree of privacy. To stop apps from showing up in the app drawer or home screen, add them to the Secure Folder and turn on the "Hide content" option.

Easy Access to Device Preferences

To swiftly access device settings, swipe down from the top of the screen using two fingers. By using this shortcut, you can bypass the notification panel and get straight to the Settings menu.

Easily View the Notification Panel

From anywhere on the home screen, swipe down to reveal the notification panel. Without having to extend your thumb to the top of the screen, you can quickly access notifications, fast settings, and other helpful information with this shortcut.

Utilize Two Messengers for Different Accounts:

To operate two independent accounts in separate
messaging apps at the same time, use Dual Messenger.
Go to Settings > Advanced features > Dual Messenger,
turn on Dual Messenger, and choose the apps you wish
to duplicate.

Wireless DeX and Mirroring Screens

Use screen mirroring to wirelessly project the screen of
your device onto compatible smart TVs or monitors. As
an alternative, you can utilize Wireless DeX to emulate a
desktop environment on a larger screen without using
any wires with your device.
S Pen Quick Translation:

To swiftly translate text on the screen, use the Air
Command menu on the S Pen. To translate a text, just
move the S Pen over it, pick the target language from the
Air Command menu, and then click the Translate option.

Discover these hidden gems and quick tips to improve the effectiveness, convenience, and fun of using your Samsung Galaxy S24+. Try out several features to find new ways to optimize and personalize your device to meet your needs.

8.2. How to Get the Most Out of Your Samsung Galaxy S24+'s Battery

With these suggestions and techniques for maximizing energy utilization, you may prolong the battery life of your Samsung Galaxy S24+:

Turn On The Battery-saving Mode

When the battery life of your smartphone falls below a predetermined level, switch on Battery Saver Mode to prolong the life of the battery. Battery Saver Mode minimizes power usage by reducing performance, limiting background activity, and adjusting settings.

Modify The Brightness Of The Screen

Reduce the brightness of your device's screen to save electricity. To maximize visibility while preserving battery life, use the Quick Settings menu's adaptive brightness or manually change the brightness levels.

Put Dark Mode to Use

To minimize battery consumption on smartphones featuring OLED displays, turn on Dark Mode. By applying a dark color scheme to system interfaces, Dark Mode prolongs battery life by lowering the amount of power used by individual pixels.

Control the screen timeout

Reduce the screen timeout duration so that the display turns off on its own after a certain amount of inactivity. To save battery life, reduce the amount of time that the screen is active by setting a shorter screen timeout interval under Settings > Display > Screen timeout.

Minimize Background Activity

Stop apps from using up battery life by not allowing them to run in the background needlessly. Settings > Apps > [App Name] > Battery > Background usage restrictions is where you may review and control background activity for individual apps.

Optimize App Battery Usage

To find and fix power-hungry apps, track and control each app's battery usage. To monitor app battery usage data and optimize power utilization for optimal efficiency, use Device Care's Battery section.

Disable Extraneous Connectivity Features

When not in use, turn off Wi-Fi, Bluetooth, NFC, and GPS to reduce the amount of battery drain from these connectivity services. To save battery life, turn on airplane mode or use power-saving options to temporarily block all wireless connections.

Make Use of Power-Saving Modes

Utilize power-saving settings like Ultra Power Saving Mode, Power Saving Mode, and Adaptive Battery to increase battery life when using the device for extended periods of time or when the battery is low. These modes modify the settings of the device to minimize power usage and give priority to necessary operations.

Enhance Location-Based Services

To reduce battery drain from GPS usage, make optimal use of location settings and use location services sparingly. To save battery life, use location modes that save battery life or use location services sparingly.

Update your software and apps

Update the software and apps on your device for best performance and battery life. Updates with optimizations and enhancements to lower power usage and increase performance are frequently released by developers.

You may lengthen the time between charges and enhance the battery life of your Samsung Galaxy S24+ by putting these tips and tactics into practice. Use these suggestions in your day-to-day activities to maximize power use and guarantee a more dependable and long-lasting battery life.

8.3. Boosting Samsung's Performance

Use these pointers and strategies to maximize speed, responsiveness, and general efficiency on your Samsung Galaxy S24+:

Close Any Background Apps

To increase system efficiency and free up system resources, clear background programs on a regular basis. To inspect and end background apps utilize the Recent Apps page; to maximize efficiency, use the Device Care function.

Activate the Developer Options

Enable Developer Options to get additional settings and performance improvements. To activate Developer Options, navigate to Settings > About phone > Software information. Then, tap "Build number" seven times. To improve performance, change parameters like GPU rendering, background process limit, and animation scale.

Enhance Application Preferences

Adjust the app's settings to reduce resource use and maximize performance. Examine each app's options to turn off unused features, establish a background activity restriction, and fine-tune performance parameters for maximum effectiveness.

Empty the Cache and Data

To get rid of temporary files and free up storage space, periodically clear the cache and data for your programs. Select the app by going to Settings > Apps, then select the choices to remove the cache or data. When cleaning data, exercise caution because user data and app settings could be lost.

Employ Performance Modes

Utilize the performance modes on your device to adjust its performance to your needs. To optimize CPU speed and responsiveness, enable speed Mode or High Performance Mode under Settings > Device care > Battery > Power mode.

Track Battery Usage

Determine which apps affect performance and waste the battery and fix them. To examine energy usage data and optimize power utilization, limit background activity and adjust settings for power-hungry apps using Device Care's energy section.

Enhance System Configuration

To enhance responsiveness and performance, modify the system parameters. Optimize performance without compromising usability by adjusting display settings, screen resolution, and animation speed.

Update your apps and software

Update the software and apps on your device for best compatibility and performance. To install the most recent software updates and app updates, either enable automatic updates or manually check for updates under Settings > Software update > Download and install.

Restrict Live Wallpapers and Widgets

To save CPU and battery life, utilize as few widgets and live wallpapers as possible on your home screen. To improve efficiency and save system resources, pick static wallpapers and keep the number of active widgets to a minimum.

As a final option, a factory reset

Try a factory reset to return your device to its original factory settings if performance problems still occur after optimization attempts. To prevent data loss, make a backup of your data before doing a factory reset.
You can maximize the speed, responsiveness, and efficiency of your Samsung Galaxy S24+ for a more

seamless and pleasurable user experience by putting these performance-enhancing techniques and methods into practice. Try out various configurations and adjustments to see which combination best suits your requirements and usage habits.

CHAPTER 9

EXPLAINS HOW TO CONNECT YOUR SAMSUNG GALAXY S24+ TO OTHER DEVICES.

Numerous connectivity choices are available on your Samsung Galaxy S24+ to enable smooth communication with other devices. Here's how to link your gadget to additional devices and accessories:

Bluetooth Interaction

Connect your Galaxy S24+ to Bluetooth-capable gadgets, like vehicle music systems, speakers, headphones, and smartwatches. To find nearby devices to pair with, go to Settings > Connections > Bluetooth, turn on Bluetooth, and choose "Scan."

Wi-Fi Accessibility

For smooth connectivity and fast internet access, connect to Wi-Fi networks. Navigate to Settings > Connections > Wi-Fi, flip on Wi-Fi, and choose a Wi-Fi network from the list that appears. If prompted to connect, provide the network password.

Near Field Communication, or NFC

Just tap your device against another NFC-enabled device or NFC tag to instantly share content, make payments, and pair with compatible devices using NFC. To utilize NFC, make sure it is enabled under Settings > Connections > NFC and payment, then adhere to the on-screen instructions.

USB Interface

Use a USB cable to connect your Galaxy S24+ to a PC, laptop, or other devices so that you may charge and transfer data. Connect your device to the other device's USB port using the USB cable that came with it.

Mirroring the screen and Smart View

Use Screen Mirroring or Smart View to wirelessly mirror the screen of your device to compatible smart TVs or monitors. To connect to a compatible device, swipe down from the top of the screen to enter Quick Settings. From there, choose "Smart View" or "Screen Mirroring."

Samsung DeX

With Samsung DeX, you can turn your Galaxy S24+ into a desktop computer by connecting it to a monitor, keyboard, and mouse. To connect your smartphone to an external display, use a USB-C to HDMI converter or a docking station that supports DeX.

Samsung Flow

Use Samsung Flow to quickly and easily connect your Galaxy S24+ to other Samsung devices. Install the Samsung Flow app on both smartphones and follow the setup steps to sync content, transfer files, and get notifications.

Transfer Content to Neighboring Devices

Use Nearby Share or Quick Share to share images, videos, documents, and other content with devices that are close by. To transmit content to nearby devices, select the content you wish to share, then hit the "Share" icon and select either Quick Share or Nearby Share.

AllShare Cast and DLNA

Use AllShare Cast or DLNA to stream multimedia files from your Galaxy S24+ to DLNA-capable gadgets like media players, smart TVs, and gaming consoles. To ensure smooth streaming, make sure both devices are linked to the same Wi-Fi network.

USB File Transfer Directly

Use direct USB file transfer to move files between your Galaxy S24+ and a computer. Using a USB cable, connect your device to the computer. Then, use the file explorer on the computer to access the storage on your device to move data back and forth.

You may exchange material wirelessly, connect your Samsung Galaxy S24+ with other devices, and improve your overall user experience by taking advantage of these connectivity options. Try out various connectivity options to determine the most efficient means of maintaining connectivity and interacting with your accessories and devices.

9.1. Utilizing Bluetooth and Wi-Fi for Your Samsung Galaxy S24+

With its flexible Bluetooth and Wi-Fi connectivity choices, the Samsung Galaxy S24+ can communicate with other devices and networks in a seamless manner. Here's how to get the most of Bluetooth and Wi-Fi connectivity:

Bluetooth Interaction

Pairing with Devices: To find nearby Bluetooth devices, enable Bluetooth by going to Settings > Connections > Bluetooth. Then, tap "Scan." To finish the pairing procedure, choose the device you wish to pair with from the list and adhere to the on-screen instructions.

Connecting to devices: To enjoy wireless music playback, calls, and notifications, pair your Galaxy S24+ with Bluetooth devices like speakers, headphones, smartwatches, and fitness trackers.

143

Content Sharing: You can share contacts, data, and images with other Bluetooth-capable devices by using Bluetooth. To enable your device to be detected by neighboring devices and start file transfers, turn on Bluetooth visibility.

Bluetooth Configuration: Tailor Bluetooth configuration to your tastes. Navigate to options > Connections > Bluetooth to access advanced Bluetooth options. From there, you can control connected devices, modify visibility parameters, and activate functions like contact sharing and phone visibility.

Wi-Fi Accessibility

To establish a connection with a Wi-Fi network, first enable it under Settings > Connections > Wi-Fi. Then, choose a network from the list that appears. If prompted to connect, provide the network password. To access high-speed internet, connect to home networks, public Wi-Fi hotspots, and Wi-Fi networks at work or school.

Wi-Fi Direct: Without a Wi-Fi router, connect your Galaxy S24+ to other Wi-Fi Direct-capable devices directly to engage in peer-to-peer file sharing and conversation. Go to Settings > Connections > Wi-Fi > Wi-Fi Direct and turn on Wi-Fi Direct.

To make and receive calls over Wi-Fi networks in areas with spotty or nonexistent cellular coverage, turn on Wi-Fi calling. Verify if your carrier offers Wi-Fi calling, then turn it on under Settings > Connections > Wi-Fi > Wi-Fi Calling.

Wi-Fi Settings: Adjust the Wi-Fi settings to maximize network performance and connectivity. Navigate to Settings > Connections > Wi-Fi to access Wi-Fi settings. From there, you can control Wi-Fi networks, turn on Wi-Fi scanning, and set up more complex Wi-Fi settings.

Turn on Smart Wi-Fi Switching to have it automatically alternate between mobile data networks and Wi-Fi depending on availability and signal strength. For a pleasant surfing experience, this feature guarantees constant connectivity and network transitions.

With the Samsung Galaxy S24+, you can connect to other devices, access high-speed internet, and have a seamless wireless experience by making use of its Bluetooth and Wi-Fi connectivity features. Try out various features and settings to improve connection and your overall user experience.

9.2. Connecting Your Samsung Galaxy S24+ to Smart Accessories

Several smart accessories work in harmony with your Samsung Galaxy S24+ to improve daily tasks and simplify your lifestyle. Here are some popular smart accessory connections for your device:

Wearables with sensors

To get notifications, track fitness activities, and remotely operate your smartphone, pair your Galaxy S24+ with a compatible smartwatch, such as a Samsung Galaxy Watch or another Android Wear device.
Use Bluetooth connectivity to link your devices, download the companion app from the Google Play Store, and follow the setup instructions. After pairing, you can use your smartwatch to adjust notifications, install apps, and change settings.

Wireless Earbuds and Headphones

Use wireless earbuds or headphones with your Galaxy S24+ to conveniently listen to music and make calls without using cables. Apple AirPods, Samsung Galaxy Buds, and other Bluetooth-capable headphones from other manufacturers are popular choices.

Turn on Bluetooth on your gadget and place your earbuds or headphones in pairing mode. To finish pairing, open the Bluetooth settings on your Galaxy S24+, choose the detected device from the list, and adhere to the on-screen instructions.

Wearable fitness devices and fitness trackers

To monitor your physical activity, log your exercises, and examine health metrics, sync your Galaxy S24+ with a fitness tracker or wearable fitness device. Fitbit, Garmin, and other fitness trackers are compatible options.

To pair your fitness tracker with your smartphone, download the companion app from the Google Play Store, register, and follow the setup instructions. Make use of Bluetooth or Wi-Fi connectivity to connect devices and synchronize data.

Smart Home Appliances

Utilizing compatible smart home platforms like Samsung SmartThings, Google Home, or Amazon Alexa, you can manage smart home appliances and gadgets directly from your Galaxy S24+.

Using Wi-Fi or Bluetooth connectivity, you may use the corresponding smart home app that you downloaded from the Google Play Store to control your smart home devices, set routines, and automate chores.

Auto Accessories

Use Bluetooth-enabled automotive accessories or your car's infotainment system to connect your Galaxy S24+ to enjoy hands-free calling, music streaming, and navigation.

To use features like voice commands, music streaming, and Bluetooth calling, pair your device with your car's Bluetooth system. While driving securely, manage media playing, make calls, and navigate using voice commands or the touchscreen interface.

You may enjoy a more convenient and customized user experience, increase productivity, and stay connected by pairing your Samsung Galaxy S24+ with smart accessories. To get the most out of your smartphone, investigate appropriate accessories and incorporate them into your regular activities.

9.3. Using Your Samsung Galaxy S24+ for File Sharing and Casting

Casting content to other devices and transferring files are a breeze with your Samsung Galaxy S24+. Here's how to make the most of these features:

Closely Related Share

Use Nearby Share to share images, movies, links, and more with devices that are close by. To share a file, just choose it from your device's settings, hit the share icon, and select Nearby Share. Then, to share with other nearby devices, your device will look for them.

Quick Share from Samsung

Use Quick Share to share files quickly between Samsung devices. You may rapidly share data, images, and movies with other Samsung Galaxy devices thanks to this capability. To share a file, choose it, hit the share icon, select Quick Share, and enable Quick Share in your device's settings.

Cloud storage and Google Drive

To make file access and device sharing simple, upload data to Google Drive or other cloud storage services. Launch the corresponding app, upload your files, and distribute them by creating links that may be shared or by extending an invitation to others.

Mirroring And Casting The Screen

You can cast material to compatible devices, like streaming devices and smart TVs, or mirror the screen of your device. Navigate to the Quick Settings menu, choose the device you wish to cast to, and then touch on "Smart View" or "Screen Mirroring."

Smart TVs and Chromecast

Cast multimedia files, such as pictures, music, and movies, to smart TVs or devices with Chromecast support. To cast a media file, just open it, hit the cast icon, and choose which device to cast to.

File Transfer over Bluetooth

File transfers between your device and other Bluetooth-capable gadgets are possible. Turn on Bluetooth on both devices, pair them if required, and then choose files to share via Bluetooth using the file manager.

USB Data Transmission

Use a USB cord to move files between your device and a computer. To transfer files, connect your device to the computer, turn on file transfer mode, and go to the storage on your device.

Straight Share

To swiftly share content with people and apps that you frequently contact, use Direct Share. Sharing material is made easier with Direct Share, which streamlines the process by suggesting contacts and apps based on your usage habits.

With the Samsung Galaxy S24+, you can effortlessly share files, cast content, and work together with people on many platforms and devices by making use of these file sharing and casting functions. Try out these capabilities and see which one best suits your needs for sharing and casting content.

CHAPTER 10

EXPLORING FUTURE POSSIBILITIES WITH YOUR SAMSUNG GALAXY S24+

Your Samsung Galaxy S24+ creates intriguing new possibilities for the future as technology advances. Here's a look at potential future developments:

Improved Communication

Upcoming developments in connectivity, such Wi-Fi 6E and 5G networks, will offer more reliability, reduced latency, and quicker data rates. Faster downloads, more fluid streaming, and improved online gaming will all be possible as a result.

Virtual reality (VR) and augmented reality (AR)

As AR and VR technology progresses, your Galaxy S24+ may serve as a gateway to virtual worlds filled with rich experiences. AR and VR applications will provide you new ways to explore and engage with the world around you, from interactive games to virtual travel and educational opportunities.

Integration of Artificial Intelligence (AI)

AI-powered features, such as tailored suggestions, automated chores, and intelligent voice assistants like Bixby, will keep improving the capabilities of your device. As the day goes on, your Galaxy S24+ may grow even more intelligent, predicting your requirements and offering helpful advice beforehand.

Compact and Adaptable Displays

The inventive folding and flexible display technology from Samsung might open the door to new form factors and multitasking options. Future Galaxy S series models might have displays that can fold or roll up, giving users the option of a larger screen without compromising portability.

Integration of Wellness and Health

Because the Galaxy S24+ has built-in sensors for measuring fitness data, keeping an eye on vital signs, and identifying medical issues, it may be a key tool for wellness and health monitoring. Thanks to developments in health technology, your gadget might offer tailored advice and suggestions for enhancing your wellbeing.

Integration of Smart Homes

Your Galaxy S24+ may become a key center for managing smart gadgets and automating your home as the field of smart home technology develops. Control lights, appliances, security cameras, and more from your smartphone thanks to seamless interaction with smart home platforms like Samsung SmartThings.

Sustainability of the Environment

Future Galaxy S series models might put greater emphasis on environmental sustainability by using recyclable design elements, eco-friendly materials, and energy-efficient components. Samsung's dedication to sustainability may result in products that offer cutting-edge performance at the lowest possible environmental impact.

Advanced Privacy and Security

Future Galaxy devices might include cutting-edge security features like biometric authentication, secure enclaves, and improved data encryption in response to the growing concerns around data security and privacy. For Samsung, safeguarding user information and maintaining privacy will always come first.

As you continue to discover the possibilities with your Samsung Galaxy S24+, pay attention to new developments in technology and fashion that could influence mobile devices in the future. Your gadget will keep evolving as new technology is developed, bringing you new experiences, features, and capacities to improve your digital life.

10.1. Coming Soon For Your Samsung Galaxy S24+: Features And Updates

With new features and updates coming soon to improve your Samsung Galaxy S24+ experience, stay ahead of the curve. What lies ahead for you is as follows:

Updates for software

Samsung releases software updates on a regular basis to boost security, introduce new features, and improve performance. Watch for over-the-air (OTA) updates; they could contain your device's optimizations, security fixes, and the most recent iterations of the Android operating system.

One Improvement to the User Interface:

Samsung's One UI interface is always changing to make using it easier and more natural. Aim for future One UI updates that could bring further customization choices, streamlined design cues, and enhanced functionality exclusive to your Galaxy S24+.

Camera Upgrades

Anticipate additional upgrades to improve the Galaxy S24+'s camera capabilities, such as AI-powered features, new shooting modes, and camera optimizations. Keep an eye out for upgrades that enhance camera capabilities overall, as well as image quality and low light performance.

Integration of AI

Samsung is progressively incorporating artificial intelligence (AI) into its gadgets to offer more intelligent and customized user experiences. Anticipate features enabled by AI that anticipate your needs, maximize efficiency, and improve usability in a variety of areas on your Galaxy S24+.

Optimizing Batteries

To increase the Galaxy S24+'s battery life, future updates might include technologies that optimize the battery. To optimize battery longevity, these updates may include power-saving modes, improvements to battery management, and optimizations for power-hungry apps.

Improvements in Security

Samsung is dedicated to protecting its customers' privacy and security. Anticipated upgrades are anticipated to compromise security patches, vulnerability fixes, and privacy enhancements aimed at safeguarding your device and confidential information from developing risks.

Combining with the Ecosystem

With its ever-expanding ecosystem of platforms, services, and devices, Samsung offers seamless device interoperability and integration. Anticipate upgrades that improve synergy, connectivity, and interoperability between your Galaxy S24+ and other Samsung devices, including tablets, smartwatches, and smart home appliances.

Novelty & Innovations

Samsung has a reputation for being creative and eager to push the limits of technology. Watch for soon-to-be released features and developments, ranging from state-of-the-art camera advancements to innovative display technologies, that could surprise and excite you.

Checking your Galaxy S24+ for software updates on a regular basis can help you stay informed and ready for future features and updates. You can make sure you always have access to the newest features, upgrades, and enhancements meant to improve your overall experience with your device by keeping it up to date.

10.2. Connecting Smart Ecosystems To Your Samsung Galaxy S24+

By easily integrating your Samsung Galaxy S24+ with smart ecosystems, you can fully utilize its potential. Here's how to take advantage of interoperability and connectivity:

Samsung SmartThings Compatibility

The management of smart home appliances is centralized with Samsung SmartThings. Utilize your smartphone to manage lights, thermostats, cameras, and

163

other devices by integrating your Galaxy S24+ with SmartThings. To schedule automation tasks, check the condition of your devices, and get notifications when something happens in your house, use the SmartThings app.

Compatibility between Google Assistant and Home

To operate your smart home with voice commands, connect your Galaxy S24+ to Google Home and Google Assistant. To operate compatible devices, stream music, create reminders, and retrieve information hands-free, use voice commands. Your Galaxy S24+ becomes an effective tool for managing your smart home ecosystem when it is integrated with Google Home.

Integration of Amazon Alexa

Connect your Galaxy S24+ to gadgets that support Amazon Alexa to automate your house with voice commands. To establish routines, manage smart devices, and access thousands of Alexa skills, use the Alexa app. Your Galaxy S24+ becomes an essential component of your networked home ecosystem with Alexa integration.

Device Compatibility for IoT

Discover the wide range of Internet of Things (IoT) gadgets that work with your Galaxy S24+. Numerous gadgets may be easily integrated with your smartphone, ranging from locks, sensors, and thermostats to smart plugs and bulbs. Utilize specialized applications or smart home platforms on your Galaxy S24+ to manage and keep an eye on these gadgets.

Integration of Wearable Devices

For seamless integration, pair your Galaxy S24+ with compatible wearables like fitness trackers or Samsung Galaxy Watches. Using your wearable gadget, you can monitor your fitness activities, receive notifications, and remotely operate your smartphone. Savor a seamless user experience throughout the Galaxy ecosystem.

Cross-Platform Harmoniousness

Utilize cross-platform compatibility to connect your Galaxy S24+ to products and services made by other companies. You may design a personalized and compatible smart home environment with the help of numerous smart home platforms and gadgets that enable integration with various ecosystems.

Automated Sceneries and Routines

To improve convenience and expedite daily tasks, create automated scenes and routines. You can use your Galaxy S24+ to set off events according to time, location, or sensor readings. Establish a "Good Morning" ritual, for instance, that triggers the lights to turn on, the heat to go up, and your favorite song to start playing when you wake up.

MASTERING YOUR SAMSUNG GALAXY S24+

Your Samsung Galaxy S24+ can benefit from increased convenience, effectiveness, and control over your linked devices by being integrated with smart ecosystems. Investigate the potential of interoperability and connection to build a smart home environment that suits your tastes and way of life.

CONCLUSION

To sum up, learning how to use your Samsung Galaxy S24+ well will unlock a world of customization, productivity, and opportunities. We've covered every facet of your gadget in this extensive user manual, from its cutting-edge capabilities to its flawless integration with smart ecosystems.

This tutorial has given you the information and resources to make the most of your Galaxy S24+, from the time you unpack it and start the setup process to personalizing your home screen, setting up necessary settings, and discovering the plethora of apps and functions.

You now know how to extend the life of your battery, improve performance, establish connections with other devices, exchange files, cast content, and prepare for new features and updates that will further improve your user experience. You've unleashed the full power of your Galaxy S24+ and turned it into a key center for organizing your connected existence by integrating it with smart ecosystems.

Remember that your Samsung Galaxy S24+ is more than simply a smartphone as you continue to explore and learn how to use it, it's a portal to creativity, productivity, and connectivity. Your Galaxy S24+ will empower and inspire you at every turn, whether you're taking pictures with the sophisticated camera features, keeping organized with productivity apps, or enjoying entertainment on the gorgeous display.

The Samsung Galaxy S24+ is more than simply a gadget because of its state-of-the-art technology, user-friendly UI, and seamless integration with your lifestyle. It's also your friend, helper, and doorway to an infinite world of opportunities. Accept the challenge of being an expert with your gadget and let your Galaxy S24+ to take your mobile experience to new levels.

Cheers to becoming an expert with the Samsung Galaxy S24+ and discovering an endless creative, innovative, and connected world at your disposal.

Handling Your Samsung Galaxy S24+: Concluding Remarks

Congratulations for reaching the end of your Samsung Galaxy S24+ mastery adventure! You've learned important tips and tricks from reading this extensive user manual, which will enable you to get the most out of your gadget.

The Samsung Galaxy S24+ is a potent instrument that may improve your connectivity, productivity, and creativity in addition to being a smartphone. Your Galaxy S24+ puts a multitude of options at your fingertips with its sophisticated photography functions and smooth connection with smart ecosystems.

Through the completion of fundamental tasks like initial setup, setting up preferences, and investigating capabilities like file sharing, casting, and networking, you have acquired the necessary information to maximize your user experience. Regardless of your level of experience with technology, this tutorial has given you the skills necessary to maximize the possibilities of your gadget.

Keep in mind that mastering your Samsung Galaxy S24+ is a continuous process as you continue to explore and experiment. Keep up with the most recent features, upgrades, and inventions that Samsung and the Android ecosystem have to offer. Be inquisitive, knowledgeable, and involved.

Your Galaxy S24+ is more than simply a gadget; it's a doorway to countless opportunities. Let the Galaxy S24+ be your dependable partner in all of your mobile pursuits, whether it be taking pictures, keeping track of things, or establishing social connections.

We appreciate you starting this path to become an expert with your Samsung Galaxy S24+. I hope your gadget will always motivate and enable you on all of your digital journeys. Cheers to becoming an expert with the Galaxy S24+ and discovering an endless creative, innovative, and connected world at your disposal!

Support & Resources for Your Samsung Galaxy S24+

It's critical to know where to look for trustworthy information and help as you continue to experiment with and learn how to use your Samsung Galaxy S24+. The following are some excellent resources to help you in your journey:

Samsung Support Page

For thorough instructions, frequently asked questions, troubleshooting advice, and user manuals for your Galaxy S24+, go to the official Samsung support website. In order to improve your device experience, you can download software updates, get answers to frequently asked problems, and access useful resources here.

Samsung Members App

To gain access to community forums, special content, and individualized help, download the Samsung Members app from the Google Play Store. Engage in conversations, network with other Galaxy users, and get advice from Samsung specialists.

Internet Communities and Forums

Participate in online groups and forums devoted to Samsung Galaxy devices to meet other users, exchange stories, and ask questions. Users may trade advice, troubleshoot problems, and discuss the most recent advancements in the Galaxy ecosystem in lively communities found on sites like Reddit, XDA Developers, and Android Central.

Channels on Social Media

For news, announcements, and updates about Galaxy devices, follow Samsung's official accounts on social networking sites like Facebook, Instagram, and Twitter. Participate in competitions, interact with the community, and keep yourself updated about new releases and events.

Retailer Assistance

Contact the customer service channels provided by the retailer or carrier if you bought your Galaxy S24+ from them for help with setup, troubleshooting, and warranty-related questions. To help clients with their Samsung devices, a number of retailers provide specialized support services and information.

Service Centers with authorization

For expert support and repairs in the event of hardware malfunctions or warranty-related difficulties, go to an authorized Samsung service center. For assistance with servicing choices, visit the Samsung website to find the closest service location or get in touch with Samsung customer support.

Videos and tutorials available online

Discover new features, tips, and tricks for your Galaxy S24+ by watching tutorial videos, how-to guides, and online tutorials made by IT enthusiasts and experts. Tech blogs and websites such as YouTube frequently provide comprehensive guides and examples to help you get the most out of your gadget.

Samsung Experience Shops

For a first-hand look at the newest Samsung products, accessories, and services, stop by one of the Samsung Experience Stores, which are situated in a few different locations. Talk to Samsung specialists, check out interactive demos, and attend workshops to find out more about the features and capabilities of your Galaxy S24+.

Through the utilization of these tools and support channels, you may improve your understanding, solve problems, and maintain connections with the active Samsung Galaxy community. To ensure that you have a flawless and pleasurable experience with your Samsung Galaxy S24+, keep in mind that support is always available.

www.ingramcontent.com/pod-product-compliance
Lightning Source LLC
LaVergne TN
LVHW051336050326
832903LV00031B/3582